AF473056

What the Heart Craves

2

What the heart Craves

Written by Christian Clark

To my angel who inspired me to compose what's in my heart.

Rest in heaven.

Mrs. Paula Pryce-Bremmer

Writing has always been in you. Apart of you. Flowing through you. Don't be afraid. Pick up the pen. Fill your paper with pure thoughts.

TABLE OF CONTENTS

What the Heart Craves

The excitement I had in
my heart.

The anxiousness

ran through me like a
fiend looking

for the next hit.

I loved you.

Since the first day I saw you.

Eye of the storm

Even in the severest of
thunderstorms there is
still peace when I have
you in my presence.

The passion I have for
you can't fit in my heart

It's overwhelming

Do you understand that
I yearn for you?

Do you understand that
I'm thirsty for you?

Do you understand the
love I have for you?

Strides

I have never been
hypnotized before.

Surely your stride
tossed me in a trance I
can't get out of.

Each square pavement
you've touch should
surrender to you.

Changing from dirt
from brown to gold.

Even your switch is
graceful and confident.

How?!

Am I crazy?

How is that I'm in love
with your walk?

Sunset Eyes

Your eyes.

The color of honey

They can brighten up a
Dark room.

Gazing into them every
day.

I'm trying to get you to
focus on me.

Just me

I know it's hard for you
because your distracted
by the grim perspective
of your past.

Let me show you how
it's supposed to be
done.

Let me show you how
love is supposed to feel?

Let me show you show
you how love is
supposed to look.

Essence and fragrance

The Shea butter scent
from your curly natural
hair is puts my mind at
ease.
Being this close to you
is making my heart
race.
I want to take
precautions
With your body

Treat it like a holy
temple that it is.
I know where to touch.
You don't have to tell
me.
When it comes to you,
I'm an expert
Sliding my hands
around your waist.
You turn to look back at
me
Lips grazing mine.
See.

I know how to navigate
your physical.
Perfectly in sync.
Our heartbeats on the
same rhythm.

Dreams and a nightmare

I dream better when I
sleep next to you.
It's the closest I can get
to heaven.
My thoughts when the
sunrise is supposed to
be pleasant.
It's just a reminder of
the hours I have to
spend away from you.

Terrified cause of the
world we reside in
I can't help but look at
the clock.
Minutes passing slowly.
Pure torture.
Now I'm rushing home
just to be next to you.
To hold you
To taste you
To feel you
To have your love
This is what I want.
NO. this is what I need.

Next to you every night.
To be in heaven
At peace
Away from the chaos of
the day.

Our music

Since we've met, I
wanted to taste you.
Take things "Nice and
Slow"
I'm deep inside you
with your drenched
walls wrapped around
me.
Giving me your
"Tender love"
Exploring your body
with my lips

"Kissing you"
passionately like I will
never get to kiss you
again.
"Between the sheets" is
where I want to be
I promised to "stroke
you up" until you
climaxed.
But we got to slow
down "We've only just
begun"
You bury your face into
my chest

Slow riding
Yes
Now you get the flow. I
want to "Make it last
forever"
Don't hold back.
Moan for me
Don't be shy
It's just "U and I

Picture This

I'm here for your love
and affection.

Let's not complicate
things with the
distractions of the
world.

Let's be simple.

Laugh

at the unforgettable
memories.

Loving you is easy

Because of your
simplicity

Who made you?

Who made you?
Let me know
God took his time with
you
Perfection
Lord have mercy
Immaculate.
Inside and out
Every inch I adore
Every curve I appreciate
Every moment I cherish

Black Cherry

Blacker the berry
sweeter the juice
Is that what they say?
Well then, I found the
best out the bunch
You taste better than
pure honey
Your sweet essence on
the tips of my lips.
I desire for more and
more

The sweet nectar makes
my tastes buds go crazy
It's a different
experience
A fulfilling sensation.

Slow Dance

Let's dance together
We don't need any
music
Love
guiding us
Listen to the sweet
melody.
Eyes closed
Hands joined together
We're in the heavens
now.

Dancing around the
stars
We are our own
constellations
I'm high off you
I never want to stop
Our love. Our dance

Energy

Show me that same
Energy
That I can't go a day
without you, Energy
That I can't stop
thinking about you,
Energy
That every song I hear
is about you, Energy
That call me when you
miss me, Energy

That come in the middle
of the night, Energy

That I can't breathe
without you Energy.

That "everything will
be ok" Energy

I need that Energy

Letters to Ms. Q.E

You have these eyes

It is simply hard to
explain

Actually

I do know

Your eyes are my haven

A place where I can find
warmth

A place where I can find
comfort

A place where I can find
love more abundant

Filling

100%cotton

You fill them out

Your cuff

Your thickness

Not one wrinkle

Watching you struggle

Is the best view

Damn

I just want to unwrap
you

Peeling them off

Come on out of them

One leg at a time

Butter cream

Chocolate

Vanilla

Sticky and sweet

Put your sugary
goodness on my lips

Wants

I want to kiss your wet
Lips
I want to taste your
natural
Fragrance
Open. I have been
waiting for this
Treasure

More

More

More you

More of your voice

More of your gentleness

More of your kindness

More of your
tenderness

More of your closeness

More of your heartbeat

More of your spirit

More of your care

Just more

Give me

More

Balance

My courage–My fear
My strength–My
weakness
My pleasure–My pain
My everlasting–My end
My love–My hate
My light–My darkness
My peace–My chaos
My simplicity–My
complexity

My joy–My sorrow
My angel–My demon

Sweetheart

Like they say
You are the apple of my
eye
Warm like pumpkin pie
Fresh like baked cookies
Your external icing
The aroma of you
Pulls me in
Ooohhhhh—sweet
You are the best treat

Oooohh– so good
enough to eat

Love making

Messy like crumb cake

Out of all the pastries

You are the one I want

You're the one I crave

The relief to my sweet
tooth

100 Years of Love

Seconds, minutes, hours
Love flourishing
Days, weeks, months
Love everlasting
Years, decades,
centuries
Love unbreakable
Just us
Surviving the test of
time

Shut up

Shut up... shhh

Tender whispers in my ear

I had no choice but to obey

Sweet kisses were placed

Muscles weakened

Heart in submission

For once you are the
host

Anxiety on high

Your in control

Mind surrendered

Your dominance fills
the air

I am overwhelmed

But say it again

My Beloved

My beloved
My Rock when I am not
solid
My air when I cannot
breathe
My fire when the world
is cold
My cup of water when I
am thirsty

My goddess when I lose
faith

My sunshine when
things are dark

My nurse when I am
sick

My guide when I am
lost

My love

My beloved

Grow With Me

Your touch has grown
Softer
Your laughter has
grown
Sweeter
Your love has grown
Deeper
Your intimacy has
grown
Stronger

Grow with me

Grow with me like the
blades of grass

Grow with me like the
roots of the tree

Grow with me

The Power of Love letters

Can I write you a
million love letters?

That is the only way I
know how

That is the only way I
can tell you

That the anxiety you
bring

Makes it not easy to
face you

I have always been
good with words

But I fumble around
you

Overwhelming love is
for you

It never feels like
enough

Let me tell on some old
parchment

Words will guide you
If you
Read between the lines
Our story is being told

If you listen to my voice
Through my words
It explains my heart
I'm pouring out to you

Telling you where you
can live for eternity

Ecstasy

We both know what it
is

But have you had it
before?

Have you been brought
to it?

I need to know

So I can fill your
satisfaction

Tell me your desires

So, I can explore them

Regrets

Why didn't I follow
behind you?

I had you

I had perfection

Low self-esteem
poisoned my body

Self-doubt murdered
my soul

Am I too late?

I am ready now

Will you accept that I
made a mistake

I Missed you

Not one night

Not one

Where you have not
crossed my mind

Never again

Never again

I let you slip through
my fingers

Never again

I will let opportunity
pass me by

Our Eden

Let me take you on a
journey
Where the things on
your mind
Come alive
Be with me
Unlimited adventures
Be with me
Where we can be
together

Where the impossible is
possible

Travel to a place

Where never is not in
the lingo

A place where the grass
is soft

A place where your
heart is at ease

And your mind is at
rest

No pain

No strife

God made this

For us

He saw our desires

Enjoy it

Savor it

Embrace it

182109

In tune
With what's
Written on my sleeve
Gathering the words
Trying to leave an
impression

Drink after drink

Tipsy off the thought of
what the future might
bring

Left in solidarity

I drowned myself in
emotion

Searing in the events of
the night

Staring at the ceiling

Anxious

Like a school kid

I am waiting for the
results of the exam
Dotted every I and
crossed every T

Shocking is the truth
The epic fail had to be a
lie
Questioning myself
But now I see
I should have let things
be

Untitled

The intensity that you
feel

That warm sensation in
your heart

Your fire ignited

Your flame has been off

The raging storm that
you see

Thunder rocking your
mind

The rainy days have
plagued you

Clear skies, now you
can see the right path

Ease your mind

Relax your heart

Lay your worries down

Sunny, cool crisp days
are ahead

Prep

Let me prep you for
what's about to happen

Ready to play with your
soul

With my steady hands

Prepare to moan

Kissing the places I've
never seen

Subtle lips

Prepare to Exhale

Watch me as I travel
across your being

Smooth tongue

Prepare to Gasp

I'm going to take my
time

Explosion delayed

Prepare to wait

Where only in the
preparation stage

It's here

It's here

When you look for it

It's here

When you hope for it

Don't be shy

Don't be afraid

Because it's here

It's here how you like it

My love, it's here

My comfort, it's here

It's here

Here to stay

Literature sex

Making you wet with
words

Love making on a bed
of letters

Sex lasting like a run-on
sentence

Like a passionate
paragraph

No need to edit
anything

Here comes the climax

A perfect conclusion

D.D.P.S

I can see you in deep
description

No face

Just inner aura

A view of the galaxy

Celestial darkness

Your filled

silhouettes

I don't know who you
are

But you're familiar like
the palm of my hand

I've been here too many
times

Your qualities that
stand out

Like massive planets

All of your
imperfections hidden

Intent that's unforgiven

Its motive disguised

Red

You are the heartbeat
That keeps me alive
You are the sweetest strawberry
That's satisfies my sweet tooth
You're one of the rarest rubies
That's widens my eyes

You are a Rose
sprouting from the
Earth

That makes my garden
heavenly

You are a glass of Pinot
Noir

Bringing me joy with
every sip

Obstacles

Rocky roads and
treacherous streets
Love keeps me
marching
Crowded highways
Love keeps me driven
Large lakes, running
rivers,
Uncrossable seas,

And tremendous
ocean's

Love keeps me treading

Steep hills and
terrifying mountains

Love keeps me climbing

Godly obstacles

Between us

Yet love keeps us close

Destination

There's a place between
your heart and heaven
Where things are calm
Yet filled
With malice and chaos
Where things are rich
and fruitful
Yet
I'm starving for more

Where things are made
easy and simple

Still I'm finding all the
complications

Pray we are guided

Guided to the right
destination

Intoxicated

When your high
The bed seems bigger
When your high
The sheets feel softer
When your high
The melody is louder
When your high
The grip is tighter
When your high

The eruption is stronger

No more

I'm going to die loving you

Death would be my greatest adventure

Maybe I will find the answers after I reach there

To why things never worked out

Why you were never
capable of loving me?

Those answers are null
and void

We will never know

Never know the passion

Never know the
intimacy

Our love that could
have been.

Setting sail

I put your name in a
diary of lost dreams

This voyage has made
me weary

This journey ends here

My love for you has
been laid to rest

Cast into the sea

Deep into the
unexplored memories

A precious treasure

Gone

Never to be caught
again by

me

www.ingramcontent.com/pod-product-compliance
Ingram Content Group UK Ltd.
Pitfield, Milton Keynes, MK11 3LW, UK
UKHW040002200726
13854UKWH00001B/3

9 781716 158919